To Em, Kelly, Brynja, Andrea, Jackie, Jane, and the company of women with whom we have shared our time, troubles and triumphs around the kitchen table.

To Rodger, Jake, David, Tully and Wayne, the beloved guys for whom we stir the pot.

Book design team: Lynne Bowman, Elise Huffman,
Jane Bolling (cover design), and Dori Felton Ward

www.deidrehall.me

Why this book (unlike us!) looks so cheaply done

If it looks just a tad flimsy inside, it's because we've
tried hard to make it as "green" as possible. Soy ink, that kind of thing.
The paper is a bit thin, in addition to being recycled, because a thin sheet
uses way less material than a more substantial sheet of paper.
Which is a swell metaphor, when you think about it.
Most of us can benefit from being just a bit less hefty, can't we?

KITCHEN
Deidre Hall's
CLOSEUP

fast
frugal
fabulous

food
secrets

with LYNNE PARMITER BOWMAN

Who Are These Women and Why Do They Think Anybody Needs Yet Another Cookbook?

Deidre Hall is a perfectly nice, well-brought-up person who started life, as many of us did then, with absolutely no clue as to where her future might lie. She was thinking she might have a talent for hairdressing. She knew she wanted love, happiness, and babies, but because she was a blonde with no plan, she began modeling, took some acting classes, and the next thing she knew, she'd been all over the TV screen for several decades, perhaps best known as Dr. Marlena Evans on NBC's long-running *Days of Our Lives* daytime drama. She also—very intentionally—became a mother of two sons along the way, David and Tully, and is still hard at work on the happiness and love part.

Lynne Bowman met Deidre in about 1968 when Deidre was modeling and Lynne was an art director for Redken Laboratories. Lynne hired Deidre for a print job, and by the end of the shoot, they were best pals and still are. Lynne had a long career, ultimately as an advertising creative director, and now does community work in her adopted hometown, Pescadero, California, where she actually spends most of her time cruising around in a red Chevy pickup pretending to be a cowgirl. Lynne has somehow managed to stay married to the same man, Rodger, for more than twenty years, (maybe it's the food?) has a son, Jake, two daughters, Kelly and Brynja, a rock star son-in-law, Wayne, and the world's most spectacular grandchild, Helen.

Together, Deidre and Lynne have been getting into trouble and making hideous mistakes in and out of the kitchen for so many years now, they've finally started to get the hang of it. In fact, they now think they're pretty hot in the kitchen, and are delighted to share their hard-won wisdom with anyone who will pay attention.

So, on the following pages, when you see that editorial "we," it's *us*.

Deidre's Introduction

My son David's first spoonfuls of solid food, cereal, followed by Tully's two years later, were the beginning of my food consciousness. Until then, French fries were a vegetable, toffee and Parmesan popcorn were staples, and a weight loss program meant skipping lunch. (It worked at 23!) My beloved boys came to me late in life, as did my nutritional awareness.

When the boys were in elementary school I complained about the school lunch. I was told, in the nicest possible way, "If you don't like it, change it." That change came with much distress and the pleadings of my little ones. "Why? What's wrong with cookies and cupcakes at lunch? Why do YOU have to do it? The kids are mad at me!"

It was my first brush with activism that continues to this day. David and I flew to Washington, D.C to ask members of Congress to renew and improve the Child Nutrition Act, and I have joined Elizabeth Kucinich's efforts to include more plant based, locally grown foods in our school lunches.

I planted a garden when the boys were quite small so my children wouldn't think their food grew in tidy rows at Gelson's grocery store.

One constant of the last forty years has been my friendship/kinship with Lynne. We have supported each other through joyous and devastating times, financial ruin, crushing betrayal, and exquisite success, all issues made manageable with time at the kitchen table. Lynne is, simply put, my friend.

I mention the kitchen table since this is where many a plot has been hatched ("Let's bake him some banana bread!") This book began a hundred times over the past several years with Lynne at the stove or poring over time-tested family recipes as I wielded legal pad and pencil. It would be bumping along wonderfully well until the next interruption came: "It's the new J. Crew, Restoration Hardware, Country Home catalogue," "Was there any cake left over from last night?" or "The DOGS/ CAT/ HORSES are out!!"

We're happy to finally be able to invite you to pull up a chair, as we present to you our labor of love, with gratitude to our brilliant and courageous predecessors, the producers of FOOD, Inc., *Jamie Oliver's Food Revolution*, Dr. Oz, and others we spoke of in the book. And in case you were thinking all we dish about is food, just wait for our next books!

Deidre

Contents

"I'll Have What She's Having?"

How do those women you see on the tube year after year, decade after decade, keep it glued together? What in the world are they doing so they still look eerily like they did when you used to watch the show every day in the eighties with your Grandma? Great question. We'd like to offer, with utmost humility, a few answers. Not that we know a huge amount more than you do. The difference just may be that because it's our business, we pay very close attention to this stuff, and try it out if we think there's a chance it's going to make us look a little better or feel a little more energetic. If it seems to work, even a little bit, we practice it, and maybe in some cases perfect it. If it doesn't work for us, we not only reject it, but tell everybody we know it didn't work.

Now, we want to share with you what did work, hoping you'll have some fun doing your own personal research on the matter.

When you're in front of the camera every day, year after year, the environment is extremely unforgiving.

If you think your boyfriend or your grown daughters are a tough audience, try going out in front of folks who have been watching you carefully, close up, every day of the week, on the tube since 1976. Hair color not quite right this week? You'll hear about it from the wardrobe guy, the producer, your fellow actors, and TV-watchers all the way from Dubuque to Dubai, not to mention your sister, your Mom, and your pal in San Francisco. *("Aaaaaaugh! What were you thinking! It's so dark! The highlights are all wrong!")*

If you missed the broadcast, all you have to do is go to the grocery store, and it's right there in the checkout line, all over the tabloids: "Soap queen washes out with too-dark hair and 20 extra pounds!" or "Daytime Diva Dives into Deep Despair, Drowns Sorrows in Doughnuts."

If you're going to survive with so many eyes on you from every direction, you learn a few things about makeup, hair, and wardrobe. You learn—sometimes painfully—how to keep your body in decent shape with exercise, and you learn how to eat to keep your energy up and your weight down, even when you have to leave the house at 6 a.m. and work an 18-hour day.

The good news, then, is that you've kept your job and your audience for a few years. The bad news is that the longer you succeed and the older you get, the more you have to keep learning it all over again. And again. And again.

You change, obviously, as you age; your nutritional needs change, and your level of activity changes. The world of information changes, too, and while some things—actually, lots of things—your grandma knew to be true about food are still true, we have learned some important new information along the way. How do you sort through all of it?

Just about the time you think you might have it figured out, some new doctor or diet guru comes along on the morning shows and announces that everything you thought you knew about food is now wrong. Eggs? No! Too much cholesterol. Whole grains? Too many carbs. Dairy products? Too many allergens.

So you stop eating eggs, refuse to cook your husband's favorite omelet, lecture your kids or your pals about all of it, and what happens? You *know* what happens. The very next week, you've got the morning show on again (while you iron that blouse, clean some goo out from under the sink, review your stock options and knock off some ab crunches) and the very latest Dr. Ladeedah Guru is on with her new book. She's slim and radiant and confident, and she's telling the world that everything we knew for sure last week about eggs (or carbs or dairy products or whatever) is no longer true. Now, this week, it's okay to eat eggs, as long as the chickens are free and happy and eat a vegan diet and have graduate degrees from good colleges.

So, dear pals, we've tried to sort that out, for ourselves and for you. We're hoping you'll toss this little book in your bag and take it with you on your rounds, to help with the truly big questions in your life:

"What the blazes am I gonna buy at the grocery store?"

"What the blazes am I gonna cook tonight?"

"What the blazes should we really be eating?"

Which, strangely, leads right into

"Who the blazes am I, anyway?"

But that's another book.

Only the Best

Along with lots of those diet experts you've heard entirely too much from, we do want to chime in on one thing: *enjoy* your food. In fact, we think you should dine like a fricken' *movie star* at every meal—hence this book. What exactly does that entail?

Attitude.

We want to suggest that you adopt a major 'tude, if you haven't already, that you deserve nothing but the very best: the most beautiful, the most delicious and the healthiest. It may take a little practice to work yourself up to Full Diva, but we want you to consider starting with some little things that will help set the tone for you.

Truffle salt. It's expensive: at this writing, something slightly upwards of twenty bucks for a little tiny container. You can buy black truffle salt or white truffle salt; either one is sublime. A few shakes, and the most ordinary omelet or pasta dish, the most inane little vegetable soup, is suddenly transformed into something truly heavenly. It's a powerful scent and flavor, so just a bit goes a long way. Not everyone loves it. But if you do, (and boy, we do; Lynne never goes anywhere without it) it's truly a bit of culinary magic.

Truffle oil. See paragraph above, but when your truffle fix comes in oil, it needs to be kept cool and has a short shelf life. Plus, you can't take it on an airplane in your carry-on bag.

Smoky salt. Our favorite is an applewood-smoked beauty from Yakima. Now, obviously, if salt doesn't agree with you or you're having blood pressure issues, you'll want to skip this paragraph. But if you do like salt, get *good* salt that actually adds more than just sodium to whatever you're preparing. A good smoky-flavored salt is terrific, for example, on a salad made with tomatoes and lettuce, because you get the fragrance and taste of bacon—subtle, but definitely there—without the bacon. Now, when you go to buy this stuff at your local gourmet or organic food store, we don't want you dropping into a dead faint when you see the price. (How much?? For SALT??) Just think of it as an excellent investment in your personal glamour.

And all those other salts. If you're going to use salt, by golly, make it good. And how lovely they look on your table: grey smoky salt, speckled truffle salt, pink Himalayan salt, red Hawaiian salt. Next time you have ten minutes (we can dream!) just look at all those little jewels on the shelf at Williams Sonoma or some other lahdeedah kitchen store. Treat yourself to at least one.

Artsy cold-pressed olive oil. Artsy is not the brand, mind you, it's the attitude. Olive oils are just like wine in that they are best when made by people who are proud to put their name on the bottle. They can be as different from one another as wines are, and some are so good that they are all you need, all by themselves, to dress a salad or pasta. Your local Farmers' Market is a good place to do some tasting, and you might even get to meet the guy or gal who's growing the olives and squishing them into oil. If it is a fresh, locally cold-pressed olive oil, in addition to being wonderfully delicious, it's a terrific thing to put into your body for all kinds of reasons we don't have time to go into here.

Enjoy the smell, the color, the flavor, and the way it makes your skin glow. No, it's not cheap, but a little money spent on great olive oil is money very well spent. And because you spent so much on it, be sure to store it either in the fridge or some other cool spot, away from your stove or heater. Real food, unlike packaged food, will deteriorate fairly quickly if you don't store it tightly sealed away from heat sources.

If your mom is sniffing around in your cupboards, finds it and demands to know how you can afford to indulge yourself with grotesquely expensive olive oil, just tell her it was a gift. It *was* a gift, from your fabulous self to your fabulous self.

These indulgent consumables do make *perfect* gifts, because you never have to worry that someone already has the same salt or extravagant lemon olive oil made by singing monks in the hills behind Cucamonga, and you're reminded of your loved one at every meal.

Remember, dear pals, the better your ingredients, the less you have to do to them.

The Big "C"

It's hard to think of a word that strikes so much terror into our hearts, and has been the subject of more confusion and misinformation. *Calorie*. AAAAAAUUGH.

There actually is some new research around the idea that all calories are not in fact totally equal, but don't you trouble your adorable little self about that. For the most part, there's no way around it. If you take in too many calories, they land right on your butt. Or your waist. Under your arms and chin. You know this. By the time you reach adulthood on this planet, you've probably read sixty books on the subject. You can read all you want, baby, but that's not gonna change the fact that every single calorie you take in that you don't burn up, you will *wear*. AAAAAAAAUGH.

If you're an average size female adult, not nursing, not pregnant, you should be taking in between 1,200 and 1,800 calories a day; a little more for guys, and more for athletes. This is not a *weight loss* diet, darling: this is how much a human body will use up every day so as not to store fat. That amounts to roughly two of those giant cinnamon rolls they sell in the mall: 1,600+ calories. One serving of Macaroni Grill's Double Macaroni and Cheese: 1,210 calories. Two Starbucks Venti Blended Cremes: 1,500+ calories. Yes, you read that right. And if you've ever ordered a Venti Blended Crème, dearest darling sweetie baby, maybe you want to read this aloud to yourself a couple of times: *two of those puppies total up to more calories than you should be eating in a whole day*. Ouch.

Those ordinary foods we grab on the run and carry around in our drink holders and feel perfectly entitled to (after all, we're hungry! We've worked hard! If we have to pick up the dry cleaning, at least we're going to have a little treat!) are hideously, grossly more than our bodies can handle, not to mention totally lacking in nutritional value.

We'd like to suggest a bit of re-framing here, as you recover from the shock of thinking about what you ate (in addition to that Venti Blended Bomb) last Thursday when you and your sister stopped by the bakery for a "little treat." Instead of thinking of your shrinking caloric requirements as a problem, a bad thing, why not think of it as a clever genetic adaptation your body benefits from? Why not see it as just the excuse you need to do all the things everyone should be doing anyway? And we use the word "shrinking" advisedly: the older you get, dear pals, the less your body needs, even if you are active.

You have been equipped by millions of years of human evolution (or God, depending on your point of view—or both?) to survive on practically nothing—twigs and leaves! Which would be so very cool in a post-apocalyptic situation, wouldn't it? But of course, *not* cool when everyone around you is chomping on chocolate croissants, macaroni and cheese, and sucking down Frappahoochies.

Here's the important other part you need to know: if you find some smart alternatives, you will become the slender, fit, healthy envy of your french-fry-chomping, Double-Frappadoodle-drinking buddies.

But wait, here we go again, ranting about fast foods, when what you want to know is what CAN you eat? What should that 1,200 to 1,800 calories a day look like and where/how are you going to get it?

If you have weight to lose, you have to keep your daily total calories under 1,300–1,500 until that weight is gone.

No, there is no way around it. Sorry. Go ahead and exercise your brains out—that's great, and necessary for good health—but you *still* have to limit calories.

The good news is that if you're eating the right kind of food, this will be plenty. You won't be hungry. You'll feel way, way better, have more energy, better skin, happier guts, and *better numbers on those pesky cholesterol and blood glucose tests*.

Plus, if our pal Jane is any example, the next time you go and get your eyes checked, you may get a much better report. It is absolutely true that eating more dark greens can slow down macular degeneration and other "aging" eye problems but don't come whining to us wanting clinical evidence—we're only qualified as TV doctors, remember. Go and look it up yourself. Google it, ferpetesake, then go make something terrific with kale. (See pages 44, 56, 66, 67)

What to Eat

- *Mostly fresh, raw vegetables,* the more colors the better. As much as you want, and at least three or four servings a day.

- *A couple of servings of cooked vegetables* every day. More is good, but don't smother them in fat: steam or nuke them with as little water as possible.

- *Whole grains.* One or two servings a day if you're watching your weight; if not, up to about six servings. Whole wheat, millet, barley, oatmeal, quinoa, or any of the other options you can find that are truly whole grains.

- *If you eat meat,* keep it to a few ounces a day and make it lean. Fish, chicken, lean pork and beef, low fat cheeses. Buy the best quality grass-fed meat you can, local if possible.

- *2 or more fresh fruits every day*, or cooked fruit with no sugar added.

- *6 or 8 nuts every day*, or more if you don't eat meat.

- *A little good oil* (olive, walnut, etc.)

- *Lots of water and tea* to drink, especially green tea. Have some coffee in the morning, but make it black or nonfat and sweeten with non-calorie sweetener.

- *When you misbehave, do it with really good, really dark chocolate and a glass of good wine.*

Eat food. Mostly plants.
Not too much. —*Michael Pollan*

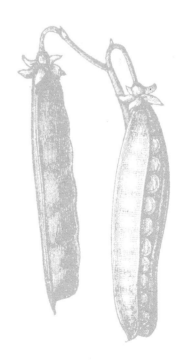

Awrighty then. That's it. That's what you get.

Oh, you're saying, wait a minute, what about white rice? What about my favorite pasta? Grape nuts? Cornflakes? Sorry, Honey. Read the labels carefully. If you still really, really want to eat those Happi-os, measure how much you pour in your bowl, and don't forget to add up how much sugar, calories and fat you're gonna pour all over 'em. Ouch.

What about that food pyramid the US Department of Agriculture puts out? Sorry. It's improving, somewhat, but still mostly for people who are okay looking like a pyramid. Unfortunately, over the years, most of the government-issued guidelines are less about what is truly healthful and more about what a bunch of overweight guys in bad suits decided was good for the Big Ag companies they represented in Washington, DC. If you doubt that for a moment, call your local public school food service provider and familiarize yourself with what public schools are required, by law, to serve kids. YUCK. We didn't want to dwell on it here, because, frankly, it's SO not glamorous.

How About Those Pesky Carbs?

If you're serious about getting your weight where it needs to be, or serious about getting out of diabetic or "pre-diabetic" territory, your carbohydrates should all come from fresh fruits, vegetables and whole grains. *Really* whole grains, not processed grains dressed up like whole grains in a healthy-looking package with pictures of smiling, politically correct people on the front. Just read the label. You're a grownup. You will very quickly figure out, if you haven't already, what is whole grain and what is marketing.

Your head reels. How can you plan meals? After all, if you open a magazine and look at the recipes, most of them start with flour, sugar and butter. What's on the cover of these magazines? Usually a cake. Check it out next time you're at the newsstand. If it's not a badly behaved actress, (some of our best friends!) it's a cake.

Tune in Martha or Rachel for a little TV food action, and what will you see? Sugar, butter and flour, right up on top. Paula Deen? Sugar, butter, flour and mayonnaise. We love these women, and are openly envious of their success, (Martha, Paula, Rachel, you *rock*, girls!) but as far as one's finely-tuned, extremely efficient body is concerned, what they're selling is food porn. And as our Aussie megastar idol, Dame Edna, would say, "we mean that in the most loving, caring way."

It doesn't take a genius to make something yummy out of cream, sugar and flour. Your mission is to know how to make something fabulous, worthy of a true hedonist, a star, out of What You Can Eat.

You notice we did say "how to make." That's because if you're going to eat really, really well, you're going to have to spend a little time in the kitchen. Not tons of time. *Some* time. You're going to have to chop some stuff, and wash some stuff, and pay some attention to all of it. Otherwise, no matter how many times you open that fridge door and stand there looking pathetic, nothing will appear on the shelves. Believe us, we've tried it, lots of times. *Nothing*.

Get used to the idea that if it comes in a package with an enticing photograph on it and a list of more than three or four ingredients, you should probably not be eating it or feeding it to anybody you like.

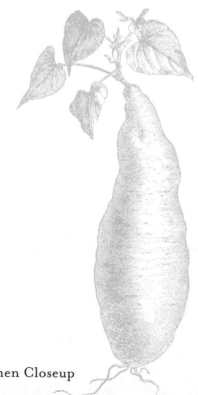

Make Some New Friends in the Produce Department

Jicama, for example, a crisp root vegetable, brown on the outside, white inside, is high in potassium and makes a swell snack if you cut it up and dip it in something healthy. Gorgeous dark green or purple **Kale**, another of our favorites, is high in flavonoids, and can go in lots of dishes, both cooked and raw. **Sweet potatoes**, high in beta-carotene, are super easy to just throw in the oven and bake. **Rainbow chard**, definitely not just for grandmas any more! It's so beautiful you want to keep it out just to look at it.

Not that you need to trouble yourself too much about exactly what beta-carotene is, or flavonoids or potassium. By all means, read up on all that in some other book (see our list, page 33!) if you're inclined, but here's the short, cinematic version: *intensely colorful foods are great for you.* White, brown and grey foods, not so much. There are exceptions, like jicama, but if a food is dark or bright green, intensely red, orange or yellow, purple or blue/black, it's probably good food. If you look down at that plate, preparing to take a bite, and all you see is beige-to-brown, you're in trouble.

The Clean Fifteen

These are the ones that the U.S. Food and Drug Administration and the U.S. Department of Agriculture tell us are less likely to have significant traces of pesticides, so you may not need to pop the extra money for "organic."

Onions	**Kiwi fruit**
Sweet corn	**Sweet peas**
Avocados	**Watermelon**
Mango	**Cantaloupe**
Pineapples	**Sweet onions**
Cabbage	**Sweet potatoes**
Eggplant	**Grapefruit**
Asparagus	

When you read the official language, however, you may still be slightly queasy about it all, and just head straight for your own backyard garden or the nearest farmers' market: "The government says that consuming pesticides in low amounts doesn't harm you, but some studies show an association between pesticides and health problems such as cancer, attention-deficit disorder and nervous system disorders."

Hmmmm. Not exactly confidence-inspiring, eh?

What Not to Eat

This is a summary of foods people are worrying about these days for various good reasons.

- ❧ *Anything with high-fructose corn syrup in it*, or with any form of sugar in the first three ingredients. We're not going to go into a giant rant right here about high fructose corn syrup, because this isn't that kind of book, but read anything on our very beautifully edited small list of recommended sources, and you will never want anyone in your family near high fructose corn syrup again. We're reluctant to use the word "evil" about a food, because before you know it we could be sliding down that crazy-lady slope, but let's just say that if we were the kind of people who did call foods evil, high-fructose corn syrup would certainly be on our list.

- ❧ *Apples*, unless they're organic. Because apples are individually grafted from a single tree so each variety remains distinct, they don't develop disease resistance. Too small a gene pool. They are sprayed and sprayed again with pesticides. If you prefer to eat apples and not pesticides, go organic.

- ❧ *Canned tomatoes* may leech a synthetic estrogen from the can lining that's been linked to health problems.

- ❧ *Corn-fed beef.* If you eat beef, look for grass-fed instead, and read anything written by Joel Salatin or Michael Pollan to understand why it's extremely important.

✵ *Farmed Salmon*. The folks who study such things are worried about what happens when you cram a bunch of salmon together and feed them in the aquatic equivalent of a cattle feedlot. There is concern about contaminants, including pesticides and antibiotics used to treat the fish. Not to mention that the fish are probably not very happy.

✵ *Foods with a "long shelf life."* You don't wanna know what they had to do to that food to get it to last forever. And, anyway, it's *you* we want to last forever, not the pot roast.

✵ *Microwave popcorn.* Chemicals in the lining of the bag have been linked to fertility problems.

✵ *Milk produced with artificial hormones.* The growth hormone that boosts milk production also increases udder infections and other problems we won't mention here because we are talking about food, and we don't want you to slam the book closed in disgust. Let's just say if you're going to eat dairy products, it's good to know where that cow has been and what she's been eating and with whom.

✵ *Nonorganic potatoes.* They're treated with fungicides while they grow, sprayed with herbicides before they're harvested, and sprayed with another chemical after harvesting to prevent sprouting. Eeeeeeeeew.

The Dirty Dozen

According to the U.S. Food and Drug Administration and the U.S. Department of Agriculture, these twelve vegetables and fruits in U.S. markets contain more than 47 pesticides per serving. Either their skin tends to absorb more of the chemicals, or more are used in their production. So when it comes to any of these, either grow your own or pop the extra money for organic:

Celery	**Sweet bell peppers**
Strawberries	**Nectarines**
Apples	**Blueberries**
Peaches	**Spinach**
Cherries	**Lettuce**
Potatoes	

Smaller Really is More Beautiful

It's so obvious, when you think about it, but these are the words we keep coming back to when we talk about how we're going to live now:

Take bigger pleasure from smaller things.

We've been living at a time when it seemed everything kept getting bigger and bigger. Cars were huge. Homes had to be mammoth, lumbering creations. Remember those shoulder pads, earrings and hair from the eighties? Some of us (we're not mentioning names here) are still digging them out of the backs of our closets. When you sat down to a meal, it seemed right to put tons of food out and pile plates high. Restaurants prided themselves on how gigantic their servings were. Grandmas and Aunties were revered for their "groaning tables."

Well, girlfriend, that's not working so well for us any more. Earrings the size of bedroom furniture tend to come and go, style-wise, as do shoulder pads and big hair, but those giant houses and cars are going the way of the mastadon. If you care about your health, same goes for those behemoth meals.

When you're preparing a meal for yourself or a party, don't think big. Thing *gorgeous*. Think fresh. Think fragrant. Think COLOR. Don't think *large*. Take a little time and have some fun making it all *look* wonderful. Decorate your plates with a few berries, a mint leaf, some micro greens, and you are guaranteed to get a good response from whomever you're feeding.

Don't forget your eyes need to be fed, too, along with your nose and your soul.

What To Read

Don't panic. It's a short list. These are books that are going to inspire you and educate you about food. They're fascinating reads that will change the way you think about food, the way you buy food, and quite possibly help save the world. We're exaggerating, slightly, but forgive us, because we really, really want you to read these.

David Zinczenko, *Eat This, Not That!* Perfect to carry in the car. Little Brittany is whining for Krispy Kremes? Taco Bell? Just have her read aloud what the damage is for her favorite choices, and then see what Mr. Zinczenko offers as better options.

Michael Pollan, *The Omnivore's Dilemma.* A wonderfully written, readable, elegant, surprising, thoughtful book about where your food comes from. In fact, do yourself a favor and read anything Michael Pollan has written. *Botany of Desire*, for example, has also been made into a wonderful movie. Or, another swell example:

Michael Pollan, *Food Rules.* It's short, super easy to get through, and makes it all very clear. Carry it with you.

T. Colin Campbell, PhD, and Thomas M. Campbell II, *The China Study.* "...One of the most important books about nutrition ever written—reading it may save your life," according to Dean Ornish, MD, and we concur. It's not just one study, as you might infer from the title, but an overview of lots of nutrition studies that offer very conclusive results that you've probably never heard about. Campbell explains the reason we don't know about these results is that we've intentionally been kept in the dark. This fact in and of itself is an extremely interesting story. If you can only read one book about food, read this one, and then get the Michael Pollan books on CD and watch the movie. We can almost guarantee it will change the way you eat, as in "Why didn't I read this years ago?? What have I been doing to myself? My kids?"

How Your Food Day Looks

First, breakfast, every day. It doesn't matter if you're hungry when you get up, or if you're "not a breakfast person." Fabulous, healthy, energetic people (that's you, right?) eat breakfast every day, even if it's teeny. And it can be so easy.

You've probably already read those other books about how eating breakfast kick-starts your metabolism so you actually burn more calories all day. And what you're going for, as a hedonist and as a healthy, slim person, is to *never get too hungry*. A little hungry is okay. So hungry you could eat half a cow is not okay. If you're teetering on the edge of diabetes, or already way over the line and just in denial, know that hunger is not your friend. Your challenge is to eat *less food more often*.

FOR BREAKFAST, EVERY DAY: Nut butter, unsweetened, and some great whole-grain toast. You need to try and get a little protein, veggies if you want and some fruit. A couple of eggs or egg whites in some form, plus any veggies you want to add, or some yogurt and fruit. Or a small bowl of real oatmeal and fruit. Or make a smoothie full of great stuff. (Fabulous recipes to follow.) Once in a while, maybe a vegetarian sausage patty or two and fruit.

When we say "yogurt," we do not mean the stuff that comes in cheery little cups with pictures of fruit. We mean PLAIN yogurt, unsweetened, unadulterated. The best kind is Greek yogurt, which has had a lot of water drained out of it for a creamier, heavier texture. You can get it nonfat, 2% fat or whole and adulterate it yourself with agave syrup or non-calorie sweetener, if you want, or lemon juice or strawberries or whatever makes you happy.

Likewise, oatmeal. If it has a picture of happy people and gleaming, perfectly groomed fruit on the outside, or if the package has anything other than oats listed in the ingredients, put it down. Not for you. Real oatmeal usually comes in a rather plain, grimly handsome can that makes no promises whatsoever except that it contains oatmeal that has to actually be cooked.

FOR LUNCH, EVERY DAY: A salad jammed with as many colors as possible. If it's only greens with maybe some red, so be it. If you have to have a sandwich, stuff it with vegetables and have veggies and fruit on the side, and make sure the bread is something worth eating.

FOR DINNER: just make sure it includes two or three vegetables, a small amount of protein, and maybe some whole grains. Fruit? Sure. The hard part is making sure you get those vegetables in. How do you do that? Soup and a "main dish" full of vegetables. If you're eating this stuff, you really don't have any room left for much else.

What You've Just Gotta Have

It doesn't take a whole lot, but there are certain things you just have to have in the kitchen or it's not going to work. So whether you're in that place where you're throwing everything into the street except what truly matters, (like our buddy Em, who only kept what she could fit in her 14-foot trailer and took off for Puckerbrush, Nevada) or moving into your very own space for the first time, here's the scoop on what you really need.

A garden pot or two on your porch or balcony or kitchen window shelf. Grow chives, parsley basil, nasturtiums, calendulas, wheatgrass—lots of good stuff to throw in a salad or decorate a plate with.

Big ole' skillet with a lid. It's hard to beat black cast iron for the skillet, and a glass lid makes it just about perfect for everything. Cast iron is cheap, looks great in the most amazing modern kitchen or out on a cattle drive, and will never wear out. All you need to remember is no soap, ever. Just wash with very hot water and scrub it clean. Small price to pay for a pan you can cook anything in.

If you're someone who has a problem with iron, as in the doctor has said you shouldn't take in too much, get something like Le Creuset which has a coating over the iron.

Big Soup Jar. After you finish this book, you will almost certainly be making a bunch of Genius Soup every week, and you will need something to keep it in: a big glass jar that hold a gallon or more with a tight-fitting lid.

ATLAS
SPECIAL
MASON

Blender. There are pretty goods ones out there for the price of a movie ticket. You only need three speeds and "pulse," but if you want the blend-o-rama one that has the huge glass bowl and 37 speeds, get it. It needs to smush things up, not leak, and look cool on the counter if that's where it's gonna live. There are also single serving, adorable teeny blenders that let you just put a lid on what you've blended and run to the car with it.

> D: I'm a shameless fan of the "Bullet," which you can find anywhere. Fast, easy, and it just rinses clean.

Bowl. Most of us have too many, but if you want to keep it simple, just be sure you have one HUGE bowl. There's no such thing as too big. If you're doing salad or pasta you need to toss it, and you can't do that in an undersized bowl.

Butler's Friend. Cheap, small, easy wine bottle opener.

Chili Pot. We love cast iron, but any heavy pot with a tight-fitting lid will do, so long as it's about big enough for a whole chicken.

Colander. Something attractive if possible, or at least something with great character. Besides draining your just-washed produce and pasta, you can just plunk it on the table with pretty fruits or vegetables in it.

Knives. Guys seem to know this instinctively, but women (maybe for some deeply seated psychological reasons we can't even begin to look at here) resist spending a little money and time on a few good knives. If you only get one thing on this list, it should be a good knife or two. A couple of little paring knives 4 or 5" long, a serrated bread knife and a big chopping knife could be enough. Don't put them in the dishwasher and keep them sharp. If you're going to eat well, you're going to have to chop some fruits and vegetables, and if you're going to chop some things, you need a good knife or two.

Microwave Oven. It doesn't have to rotate, it doesn't have to be big, but if you don't have one, get one.

Pyrex (or other heat-proof) glass measuring cups: 8-cup, 4-cup and 1-cup, with pouring spouts.

Pasta or Stockpot. BIG is good; something you can get a gallon or more of soup in.

Salad spinner. If you're reading this book, chances are your future includes a lot of salad, and it needs to be dry before you dress it.

Saucepan with a lid that fits well. Fairly heavy, good quality, medium-sized if you only want to deal with one.

Spatula. You'll want a metal one for your big ole' skillet with a lid, and a plastic one if you're using a nonstick pan.

Spoons. You need a few spoons. Wooden, slotted, big, maybe a ladle.

D: I never use my microwave! It makes me nervous thinking about and how all those microwave rays are running amok in my kitchen.

L. Dr. Mehmet Oz thinks they're not a problem, and you think he is fabulous. He is fabulous, isn't he? He wouldn't be nuking stuff if he thought his brains would fall out.

D: I do love Dr. Oz, but I have not heard him weigh in on either side of this question. I have read Dr. Andrew Weil, Dr. Joseph Mercola, Dr. Hans Hertel and others on the dangers of microwave use as well as other EMR concerns, and I shall continue to rattle those pots and pans!!

Pantry Checklist

The idea is to stay out of the grocery store completely, if you can. Go once a week or order from a delivery service (very star-like!) and don't go at all. Your life will improve. You'll save money. You won't buy those magazines at the checkout counter. You won't run into people you feel obligated to talk to even though you're late and tired and hungry. Keep yourself stocked up with these indispensables and you'll never be without something swell to eat.

In addition to what we've listed here, you will of course be going to your local farmer's market or produce stand to pick up lovely fresh berries or apricots, fresh greens and so on. What we're listing in this section are the things you can keep on hand that won't go bad quickly.

Agave syrup. You can get it raw or otherwise. It's a natural syrup that doesn't seem to disturb systems the way sugar and sugar-like things do, and it's delicious either on its own or as a sweetener in cooking. Keep it in the fridge.

Baking soda and baking powder

Beans. Have a can or two of black beans, big cannellini beans, cut green beans, and some dried lentils, at least.

Butter-like substance or good real butter

Canned crushed pineapple. We've always got at least one or two cans, just in case we need to make an emergency *of-course-I-would-never-forget-your-birthday* cake.

Cheese. Parmesan, always; feta and goat cheese, most of the time.

Chocolate. Dark bars, cocoa powder with nothing in it but ground cocoa.

Good oil: olive, canola, walnut, etc. Keep them cool, away from the stove.

Flour. *Whole grain* flour. Bob's Red Mill is a great brand, and there are lots of others. Buckwheat flour, millet flour, spelt flour—the list goes on and on.

Nut butter: peanut and almond, at least. Make sure there's nothing in it but nuts and maybe salt. Our pal Em actually lived in her adorable little retro trailer for more than a week with nothing but nut butter, psyllium and apples, and was as happy as she's ever been. Of course she was in New Mexico at the time, and when you've got that kind of air, who needs food at all?

Nuts. Raw and/or roasted, salted or not: walnuts, almonds, pistachios, cashews, etc. Nuts have a short shelf life.

Pasta. Brown rice noodles and spaghetti

Produce that keeps well: Jicama, kale, sweet potatoes, celery, lemons, red and yellow peppers, onions, garlic, avocados, carrots, parsnips, apples, oranges

Psyllium. It's just bean husks, and a great way to add fiber to your diet. No flavor, no calories, just a little texture you can hide in nut butter, salad, smoothies, whatever. You can also use it to thicken sauces or cooked fruit without adding calories.

Salt. Always have two or three nice salts; see page 16.

> D: Nuts and nut butters, once the jar has been opened, should be kept in your refrigerator.

> L: Even then, always give them a sniff before you use them: if they've gone off on you, your nose will know.

Salsa. Red and green. Read the label! We like ours with no sugar (or evil sugar-like substances) and lots of cilantro. Herdez brand is terrific.

Spices. Cinnamon, nutmeg, curry, pepper, at least.

Unsweetened applesauce, canned. See note on crushed pineapple.

Vegenaise®. Look for it in the refrigerated departments of health food stores. It tastes better than any other ready-made mayonnaise we know and it's made without eggs.

Xylitol or similar sweetener. This is a great-tasting sugar alcohol sweetener made from the fibers of various berries, corn husks, oats, and mushrooms.

What You've Gotta Make Now

[Actual recipes of the famously frugal and impatient]

Super Breakfast Smoothie

Add your favorite protein powder (we suggest a non-dairy choice) to

½ cup almond or rice milk

½ cup fresh or frozen strawberries, blueberries, raspberries, or blackberries (full of fiber, minerals, vitamins and healing anti-oxidants! Blueberries also appear to delay the onset of age-related loss of cognitive function.)

3 tablespoons ground flax seed (Omega 3!!)

12 almonds (protein and healthy fats)

1 small handful of fresh spinach, kale, chard or other dark greens. (Do we need to tell you why?)

Thirty seconds in the blender or Bullet and done. Perfect for breakfast, or any time you can't seem to get motivated to actually cook. Great healthy, yummy treat.

Chocolate/Peanut Butter Shake

Add chocolate protein powder to ½ cup almond or rice milk

1 tablespoon peanut butter

12 almonds

½ cup yogurt (An excellent source of protein, calcium, riboflavin and vitamin B 12)

The variations are endless, and it's hard to beat the Smoothie form factor for high speed and functionality. It's a great kid/husband-friendly way to slide more fresh fruits, fresh vegetables, more liquid and more fiber into your diets. Breakfast, lunch, after school, dinner.

Dessert First

We figured we should start right after breakfast with the sweet stuff, because the truth of the matter is that's where lots of us always want to dive in.

In fact, our REAL feeling is that most meals are much better just being *replaced* with desserts. Very large dessert. Or perhaps many desserts. Gooey, crunchy, chocolaty, fruity, cakey, no matter. So long as it is really, really sweet.

If you're feeding a family, that can be a sticky wicket. But if it's just you tonight, why not? Or you and your girl-friends? Go for it. Just be sure it's good, REAL food. Instead of eating tons of it, eat slightly less, but eat it slowly and sensuously and happily, free of guilt or recriminations, just like the stars you really are.

Go ahead. You can get crazy with any of our desserts without doing yourself severe harm. If that's what you want for breakfast, or instead of dinner, by golly, that's what you should have.

Unless your kids are watching, of course. Sometimes, even if your kids ARE watching, loosen up and eat some sweets with them and make sure they know the difference between empty, sugary calories and really good treats.

Rhubarb. Really.

First of all, people, this is a pink food. Pink has a way of saying to your brain, "hey, this is fun," or maybe even "gosh, how naughty!" In fact, pink or not, it is a *leafy vegetable*, and you will be eating the stem. The only thing between you and loving rhubarb is a generous amount of your favorite healthy sweetener.

Wash the rhubarb, cut off the cruddy parts (green or brown) and cut it into two or three-inch long chunks. Put it with a little water in a pan with a lid (or if you're nuking, a suitable vessel with lid) and cook it on medium or low heat until it's soft, which only takes about five minutes on a regular stove, and way less in a microwave. Add a spoonful of psyllium if you want, and throw in plenty of your favorite non-caloric sweetener.

There ya go. Keeps a long time in the fridge. Perfectly ok to pull it out and snarf down a little when you need to. And it's a *leafy vegetable* for petesake. Just don't eat it raw, because it's toxic unless it's cooked.

Chocolate Orange Cake

This is not totally easy. In fact, if you are as hassle-averse as we are, you'll agree it's a bit of a pain in the patootie, but worth it. When you love sweets but don't love junk, your options are somewhat limited, so we wanted you to have a show-stopping number to do when the occasion calls for it. Serve it with slightly sweetened mascarpone cheese: just add a little agave syrup or other sweetener and ¾ teaspoon vanilla to an 8-ounce container of mascarpone.

Butter-like substance (like Earth Balance) or butter

1 ¼ cups whole almonds, or 6 to 7 ounces almond flour

1 tablespoon flour

1 cup sugar or equivalent

6 ounces dark bittersweet chocolate (or sugar-free) coarsely chopped

½ cup unsweetened cocoa powder

½ cup fresh orange juice

2 teaspoons finely grated orange peel

6 large eggs, separated (from emotionally well-adjusted, clean-living chickens)

1 teaspoon vanilla extract

¼ teaspoon salt

Preheat oven to 350°. Brush butter or vegan substitute generously onto the bottom of a 10" springform pan. If you're using whole almonds, blend them with ¼ cup sugar or sugar substitute in a food processor until they're finely ground. If it's almond flour, blend the chocolate and ¼ cup sugar/substitute first, then add the almond flour.

Whisk the cocoa powder, orange juice and orange peel in a small bowl until smooth. Combine egg yolks, vanilla and ½ cup plus 2 tablespoons sugar/substitute: beat with electric mixer until very thick, about 4 minutes. Beat in cocoa mixture, then fold in almond mixture. Beat egg whites and salt in a large bowl until soft peaks form (be sure beaters and bowl are perfectly dry and clean first) Gradually add 2 tablespoon sugar/substitute, beating until whites are stiff but not dry. Fold whites into chocolate batter, ⅓ at a time. Transfer batter to the prepared springform pan and bake at 350° for about 40 minutes, until a toothpick in the center comes out clean. Cool the cake completely in the pan. You can make it the day ahead, cover with foil and store it at room temperature.

Who Knew About Pineapple?

Who doesn't love pineapple, cool and crunchy and juicy, so beautiful on the plate and on the tongue? The symbol of hospitality! The fruit that doesn't need to be refrigerated until you cut it, makes spectacular table art until you're ready to eat it, and—here's the part that was recently news to us—may be very effective in helping you heal?

Huh? Pineapple? Yep. Next time you have some kind of surgery, (not that we ever do, ourselves, but of course we have good friends who, occasionally, for one reason or another, might, although that is entirely their own business, and we are not going to name names) do not be surprised if your doctor recommends that you eat a half-cup or so of fresh pineapple for a few days before your procedure (no matter what that procedure might be, elective or otherwise, and it's absolutely none of our business. We mean it.)

Pineapple has been used for centuries to treat indigestion and reduce inflammation. Bromelain, the enzyme from the stem and juice, was isolated from the pineapple plant in the late 1800s, and seems to be particularly effective in reducing inflammation associated with infection and injuries.

"Studies show mixed results," say the texts, which is usually shorthand for "nobody will make any money here, so let's move on." But why not eat some yummy pineapple anyway? It very well may reduce swelling, bruising, healing time and pain, and there is some evidence that bromelain can also kill some viruses and bacteria.

It's also full of fiber, famously good for your digestion, and makes your kitchen or dining room smell fabulous just by sitting there on your table, elegantly, sweetly, hospitably, waiting to be eaten.

Did we mention inexpensive? Gorgeous? Our favorite things! Better yet, here's the recipe for one of the best desserts you'll ever eat:

Cut the outside off the pineapple and put it on a plate.

There ya go. Done. Or, for even more glamour, dip it in some melted dark chocolate.

Mimi's 18-Carat Cake

Here's the cake you make whenever you need that killer baked item that knocks people right out of their chairs but is actually such good food that you can feed it to small children without feeling guilty. It's a perfect birthday cake even for the super-critical mommies group who food-mill everything. It's super-easy, only takes one bowl, and will keep a couple of weeks in the refrigerator if you cover it well. Leave the nuts out, if you want; nobody but you will miss them.

2 cups flour (we mix whole grain buckwheat, millet or whole wheat with some white flour)

1 ½ teaspoons baking soda

2 teaspoons baking powder

1 ½ teaspoons salt

2 teaspoons or more cinnamon

1 cup Splenda®, honey or agave syrup

1 ½ cups applesauce

4 eggs

2 cups finely grated carrots

½ cups chopped nuts (pecans, walnuts, almonds or pistachios)

3 or 4 ounces flaked coconut

1 can (8.5 ounces) crushed pineapple with juice (not enough, probably, to make this totally medicinal —see page 50, but isn't this better than the 2 cups of oil you usually see in a cake recipe?)

Sift the dry ingredients together, mix well with the sweetening and eggs, then add everything else. Pour into three 9" round pans that have been greased and floured, then bake at 350° for 35 or 40 minutes. Cool thoroughly before you frost.

Frost with mascarpone cheese, sweetened with your favorite sweetener plus a half-teaspoon of vanilla or rum for flavor.

Why Soup Comes Right After Dessert

Several reasons. First, you can make a batch, stick it in the fridge and eat it every day for a week, dolling it up to look brand new every time. It's cheap, usually, makes you feel like you've really eaten something, and, here's the best part: it's full of water. You know you're supposed to be drinking more water, but do you? Really? Truly, you're drinking enough water? We didn't think so. You have to be clever about it and sneak it in on yourself in all kinds of ways. Soup is an *extremely* clever way to get more water in, more vegetables in, fill yourself up with fewer calories, and make everyone around you feel well-fed and loved in the process.

Soup can be a first course for company or a whole meal. If you usually eat too fast and want too much (you know who you are!), soup is the way to slow down. Plus, every time you eat one of these lovely homemade soups instead of some cardboard diet dinner, you save a few bucks along with untold amounts of sodium and all that packaging.

Why, then, for petesake, aren't you eating your own homemade soup every single day? Because, we're guessing, you think it's hard to make? You couldn't be more wrong, darling pals. Everyone who eats at your table will think it was a big deal, but it is so definitely NOT. It is easy, cheap, and very forgiving.

Here are the tricks:

Most soups can use a hit of acid—lemon juice or good vinegar—if they're tasting a bit bland. The combination of a good salt and a little lemon juice can save the day.

Bite the bullet and **make a big jar of our Genius Vegetable Soup on the weekend**. Chop those fresh vegetables, get out that stockpot and do it. You will be so pleased with yourself the whole week.

Garnish your plates before you serve them, even if it's just you and your TV. Put some edible flowers, chopped cilantro or parsley, a swirl of yogurt on top, whatever is appropriate. Feed your eyes and your soul. You deserve nothing less than gorgeous and delicious at every meal. When you do this for guests, they'll think you're brilliant. We know, it's really nothing —just a nasturtium blossom on top of a bowl of soup—but it's one of those little things that's really, really huge.

L. The kitchen starts smelling great when you chop the vegetables.

D. Don't you feel like Supermom when you've got a big pot of something terrific bubbling away all afternoon?

Genius Vegetable Soup

If you only try one of our fabulous tricks, this is it. You will devote maybe a half hour, all told, of chopping and washing of vegetables, but you will reap the rewards for a week or two afterwards.

This recipe is not just for a soup, it's for communicating love.

1 cup or more chopped celery

1 or 2 onions

1 clove garlic

4 or 5 medium carrots or more small carrots

Olive oil

Vegetable broth (or chicken, if you prefer)

Canned, fresh or frozen tomatoes; 2 large jars or several tomatoes

Chopped cabbage, spinach, chard, kale, in any combination, as much as you can stuff in the pot.

Fresh chopped parsley, lemon, salt and pepper

Saute celery, onion, garlic and carrots in a tablespoon or more of oil in the bottom of a heavy stockpot until the onions are transparent. Add the broth, as much as you want, to fill up the pot about half way or more. Dump in the tomatoes and all the chopped greens and cook it for at least two hours, adding a little water or broth if it cooks down quite a bit.

When you serve it, sprinkle lots of fresh parsley on top, season it with salt and pepper and a generous squeeze or two of fresh lemon juice in each bowl.

Then, the next time you serve it, put some beans and salsa into each bowl along with the lemon, and use cilantro instead of parsley. Throw some yogurt on top.

The day after that, sprinkle some feta cheese and olives in it. Or poach fish in it, adding a little wine and olives along with the lemon and parsley.

Still got some on Thursday? Toss some brown rice noodles in with a potful of the soup and simmer until the noodles are cooked. Add the lemon, parsley and some Parmesan cheese on top. It's a whole, complete, lovely meal in a bowl, which you have prepared in seconds, practically, without harming one tiny bit of Styrofoam in the process. *Genius*.

Of course, you can just keep riffing on it, too, and come up with your own personal variations. Shrimp? Mmmmm. Or how about tossing a small bag of either cooked lentils or dried lentils, and cooking according to directions using your incredible soup base as the liquid?

We must warn you at this point, however, that you don't serve things like this to people you are casually dating and not at all serious about. Folks have been searching for centuries for potions and aphrodisiacs, when all they needed to do was make a really good pot of soup for the target of their adoration. Just please, ladies, use it responsibly, and don't tell us we didn't warn you.

Mushroom Soup

No, wait! This is really amazing stuff. It's deceptively simple, we know, but this is the old French Grandma classic, just slightly updated. Kids love this, incredibly, and you can use it just like canned mushroom soup—to make casseroles. Just try it once, and you will be our pal forever.

6 tablespoons butter or butter substitute

A sliced onion

About 12 ounces fresh crimini or shitake mushrooms

4 or more cups chicken or vegetable broth

A handful of fresh parsley

Salt (truffle or herb, maybe) and pepper

2 ounces good sherry or Bourbon

Saute the onion on medium heat in a little of the butter, until the onion is soft. Add the mushrooms and the remaining butter and continue to sauté for 8–10 minutes. Add the stock and the parsley, bring to a boil, then reduce heat and simmer for an hour. Cool it, then blend in a blender until smooth.

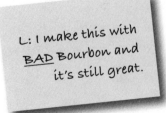

L: I make this with BAD Bourbon and it's still great.

Beauty Borscht

Even if this weren't wonderful tasting, which it is, or superbly healthful, which it is, you should make it just to see how unbelievably beautiful soup can be. It's that deep, almost translucent vermillion red you only see in roses, rubies, and once in a while, a truly fabulous retro nail polish. Gorgeous. Especially with a blop of yogurt on top and maybe a curl of orange peel.

A couple of beets, whacked into chunks

A couple of carrots

Vegetable or chicken broth—a cup or more.

An onion

Some cabbage (if you have it)

A couple of glops of yogurt

Butter (or butter-like substance of your choice)

Salt

Orange peel, vinegar or lemon juice

Nuke the vegetables in the broth (or cook them in a pot on the stove) until tender. Blend in the blender with remaining ingredients and season to taste. Reserve a little yogurt for garnish.

Carrot Soup

You can go into any number of chi-chi restaurants and order a version of this for big bucks. Or you can just make it yourself in about ten minutes and feel completely virtuous about the whole thing.

Remember to store your carrots separately from other fruits and vegetables so they don't get bitter. (Only certain fruits and veggies actually make carrots bitter, but who can remember which ones?)

4 or 5 big carrots, cut in chunks

1 cup or more chicken or vegetable broth

1 garlic clove

An onion

If you're trying to use up that zucchini squash the neighbors gave you, throw that in, too

Salt

Butter (or butter-like substance)

½ cup yogurt if you like

Nuke the vegetables in the broth (or cook them in a pot on the stove) until they're tender. (Sound familiar?) Blend in the blender with remaining ingredients and season to taste. (Are you seeing a pattern here?) Reserve a little yogurt for garnish.

Red Pepper Soup

Lynne's husband, Rodger, (the Most Patient Man in the Universe) makes this every week, not just because it's extremely easy and beautiful, but because he's got family and friends convinced that he possesses some real culinary magic. He does.

An onion

2 or 3 big red or orange peppers cut in chunks

1 clove garlic

1 cup or more chicken or vegetable broth

Some carrots or zucchini if you want

Butter (or butter-like substance)

Salt

Nuke the vegetables in the broth (or cook them in a pot on the stove) until they're tender, blend in the blender with remaining ingredients and season to taste. (Um, haven't we seen this somewhere?) Use a little yogurt for garnish, or lots of good grated cheddar cheese.

Spinach Soup

Use less liquid in this, and you have good ole' creamed spinach without all the calories and excess sodium. Use more liquid, and it's soup.

A big bag or bunch of fresh spinach or a 10-ounce package of frozen spinach

1 cup or more chicken or vegetable broth

2 or 3 ounces feta cheese

Butter (or butter-like substance)

Salt and pepper

Nutmeg—just a sprinkle, then add to taste

Nuke the vegetables in the broth (or cook them in a pot on the stove) until they're tender, blend in the blender with remaining ingredients and season to taste. (Gee, is this sounding kinda familiar?) Use a little yogurt for garnish, or lots of good grated Parmesan cheese.

Cauliflower Soup (and Sauce)

Use less liquid in this, and you have a lovely side dish to use instead of mashed potatoes. Use more liquid, and you've got a great little soup or vastly improved "white sauce" to use in mac & cheese and elsewhere.

Wait a minute, you're saying, *we're totally cheating* on this. This recipe is almost identical to the preceding four recipes! And to that we reply *Yesssss!* You're absolutely correct.

And you now have your Aha about how it works in the kitchens of the perennially fabulous. You find out how to do something really easy that works really well and then you just do it over and over again. No need to prop the recipe up and follow it slavishly. You can do this in your sleep, and heaven knows you may need to if you have small children or an early call.

1 fresh head of cauliflower

1 cup or more chicken or vegetable broth

2 or 3 ounces feta cheese (or skip this if you're not doing dairy)

Butter (or butter-like substance)

Salt and pepper

Nutmeg—just a sprinkle, then add to taste

Nuke the vegetables in the broth (or cook them in a pot on the stove) until they're tender, blend in the blender with remaining ingredients and season to taste.

Center Stage Vegetable Dishes

Even if you're a meat eater, it's great to have a couple of these in your repertoire. They're relatively cheap, which is always a fabulous idea and they're full of nutrition and color. Always a good thing!

Eggcellent Eggplant Parmigiano

2 medium eggplants

Bag of Portobello mushrooms, thinly sliced

Bag of organic spinach

Jar of organic marinara

2 packs shredded light cheese

Slice eggplant with skin on about ⅛ inch thick

In a ceramic or glass pan, spread a tablespoon or two of the sauce on the bottom. Add a single layer of eggplant, top with some cheese, then another layer of eggplant, topped with spinach, more sauce and then the thinly sliced Portobello and more cheese. Keep layering and end with a layer of the eggplant topped with sauce and cheese.

You can pre-cook the spinach and the mushrooms to eliminate a lot of the liquid that will come out. If so, get two bags of spinach as it will cook to almost nothing.

Bake at 350° (use a Silpat® silicone cooking surface so you don't need oil) for about an hour or until eggplant is somewhat soft.

If the cheese is getting brown, cover it with foil.

Important: Let it sit 15 minutes before serving. It will finish cooking as it cools.

Sneaky Spaghetti & Meatballs

You need some ideas that let you throw something on the table fast while most of your brain is otherwise occupied. Here's a surefire number you really can't mess up, and most anybody over the age of about seven can manage to make it while you do other things.

Replace your white spaghetti noodles with brown rice noodles and prepare according to package directions.

Add frozen prepared veggie meatballs and/or frozen veggie sausage to your homemade or bottled red tomato sauce and heat through.

Garnish with Parmesan and serve it.

You can also doll up the sauce and pump up the nutrition with sautéd or pureed vegetables—squash, onions, mushrooms—or fresh spinach/kale/chard, chopped, or parsley.

D: Kids love to make this, and you've given them a healthy option! You go, Mom!

L: After the initial whining, kids are happy to be totally in charge of dinner from time to time.

Pasta Verdi

These greens are easy to grow yourself and very inexpensive to buy, which is kind of crazy, because if they charged you according to how good they are for you, this dish would cost eight bazillion bucks. Don't make it because it will help stave off macular degeneration. Do not be swayed by all the antioxidant properties of the ingredients. Cook this because it is extremely fragrant and delicious and everyone will think you're brilliant in the kitchen.

Chard, spinach, kale, arugula: one or all, doesn't matter exactly how much

1 medium-sized garlic clove (in this case, size does matter: too much and you'll have a lonely night)

Green onions if you have 'em

Parsley or basil if you have them, fresh, chopped

Brown rice pasta

Teaspoon of lemon juice

Good olive oil: your very best

Salt, (truffle salt is wonderful in this) pepper

Start the water boiling for the pasta, and throw some regular salt in the pot. Chop all the greens pretty fine, so the pieces are something like ½". Don't be anal about it unless that makes you happy. Just whack it all up into small pieces and throw it in the big bowl you will serve it in. Chop the garlic very fine and throw it on top of the greens. Sprinkle the olive oil over the greens and garlic, then salt and pepper. When the pasta is cooked, scoop some of the hot water out in one of your glass measuring cups—maybe ¾ cup. Drain the pasta, then throw it on top of the greens as fast as you can, so the hot pasta wilts the greens. Toss everything together and add some of the reserved hot pasta water if it needs more liquid. Put some grated Parmesan cheese on it if you like, and use truffle salt if you like that. If you have some fresh beans, like baby limas or fava beans, throw them on top of the greens before you add the pasta.

D: When you toss salad or pasta, then serve it in the same bowl, be sure to wipe around the inside edge of the bowl with a damp cloth before you serve.

L. I prefer to use a politically correct paper towel of some kind.

Spaghetti Squash

This is not at all original with us, but it's such a classic way to make something easy and extremely healthful. If spaghetti squash is new to you, it's an actual, real-live vegetable that cooks up in lovely long strings just like spaghetti.

All you do is cut the squash is half, remove the seeds, wipe the inside with olive oil, then sprinkle with salt, pepper and cinnamon. Place it upside down in a baking pan with some water in the bottom, and bake at 350° for an hour.

When it's cooked, scrape it out of the shell with a fork, and it looks remarkably like pasta.

Top it with your favorite red sauce, or just a little butter, butter-like substance or a blop of yogurt.

It's rich in Omega-3 and Omega-6, vitamins A, B, and C and minerals.

Coolslaw

This will keep this in your fridge for a couple of weeks, which means you can open up the fridge any time and see something legal, available, relatively attractive and pretty darn yummy.

For some reason, guys love it who don't particularly like anything green, maybe because— at least in the South—it's what goes on a plate with hushpuppies, fries and a barbeque sandwich. Well, hold the hushpuppies. Hold the fries. Hold the barbecue sandwich. What you have here is crunchy, yummy, looks great (color! Texture!) and can be eaten in large amounts any time you want.

Take it with you to a potluck: it's bulletproof, everybody will like it, and you will have something there you can eat.

Chopped purple cabbage

Chopped green cabbage

Chopped red peppers (get crazy: do yellow and orange peppers, too)

Chopped carrots (if you have 'em)

Dried cranberries or cherries

Good vinegar

Good oil

A sprinkle of your favorite sweetener

Salt and pepper

Chop things as small as you like, but no bigger than about an inch long. Sprinkle the vinegar and oil over everything (a tablespoon or two of each goes a long way), then add dried cranberries or cherries (a handful or two) sweetener, salt and pepper to taste. Stir it well and let it sit before you eat it if you can.

If you want to turn it into your whole dinner, just toss some nuts in it.

Creamier version: mix a couple tablespoons of good mayonnaise or Vegenaise®. with an equal amount of yogurt and use instead of vinegar and oil.

Mexican Slaw

Here is our own version of a dish served at Duarte's Tavern in Pescadero, California. If you stop by, and please do, have it with the cracked local crab when it's in season. Otherwise, make it at home and keep it in the fridge for grabbing any time. It features cilantro, which some people love and some don't. If you are a cilantro lover, this is your slaw.

Chopped purple cabbage

Chopped green cabbage

Chopped red peppers (get crazy: do yellow and orange peppers, too)

Chopped cilantro (lots!)

Salsa Verde or canned, chopped jalapeno peppers (a few, to taste)

Good vinegar

Good oil

Salt and pepper

Toss it altogether and let it sit for a few hours before serving if you can.

Grilled Asparagus á la Binky

We're including this just so you have something brilliant to do on the grill, even if everybody around you is drowning their sorrow in pork ribs.

The sauce is nothing more than half crushed garlic (crushing garlic is hard—use the pre-crushed kind) and half Vegenaise®, scaled according to the size of the party. Something like six pounds of asparagus is not too much for a party of eight, unless you've got a hardcore bunch that won't touch anything green.

Slice the asparagus lengthwise, drip some good olive oil over it with salt and pepper, then grill until it's just barely soft. Serve it with the sauce. Some of us like to add an extra squeeze of lemon.

Diva Dinner Salad

You know those nights when you come home, wiped out, wanting something hot and yummy, but knowing what you really should have is a salad? Here ya go. It's got the hot-and-yummy part, it's a salad, and (if you paid attention to the Pantry Check List, page 40) you've got everything you need to make it.

Lettuce, green onions, tomatoes, cucumbers (or whatever salad stuff you have in the fridge)

Olive oil

Lemon juice

Salt and pepper

Ready-made green salsa (salsa verde)

Grated cheddar cheese (or good cheese substitute: we really like Daiya brand "deliciously dairy-free cheddar")

Baked tofu or your favorite garden burger patty (or a can of chicken, ferpetesake, if you're feeding someone who can't deal, otherwise)

Yogurt

Avocados if you have 'em

Toss the salad greens with lemon, olive oil, salt and pepper, and fill each dinner plate with the tossed salad. Nuke or otherwise warm the tofu, garden burger or canned chicken (or use takeout broiled chicken) with some lemon juice squeezed over it, then place the chicken on top of the salad greens, sprinkle cheddar cheese over that, top with some salsa and a blop of yogurt. If you have the avocados, either toss them in the salad or arrange them artfully around the plate.

Snax

The best way we know to get kids (or ourselves for that matter) to eat well is just to plunk the food out there before they have a chance to forage. People large and small will go for what is immediately available, so if you've got something semi-attractive ready, it will usually be devoured before anyone realizes it was a great nutritional choice.

Some favorites:

Apple slices

Pea pods

Carrots

Celery with peanut butter

Raisins

Jicama

Tangerine sections

Hummus

Strawberries

Frozen blueberries

Pineapple chunks

Frozen grapes

If it's a cool day, make peanut butter fondue with apple slices. Just melt the peanut butter and place it in a cup surrounded by the apple slices. It also works well as a breakfast treat!

For Our Meat-Eating Friends

We had some terrific chicken and buffalo (yes, really) recipes in this section, and then we suddenly went "No!"

We realized you probably have drawers full of amazing ways to prepare all kinds of meat, starting with your grandma's and your mothers' and all your aunts' favorite old recipes.

We took a quick walk through our favorite bookstore, just to build our courage up, and sure enough, there were roasts and barbecued ribs screaming from the covers of so many gorgeous, big, lushly produced cookbooks it was utterly overwhelming.

We decided we didn't want to waste one second of your extremely precious time with more of the same. What we really, really, really want to encourage you to do, and what may be the most important fabulous secret in this whole ding-dang book, is to try making more meals, or even *most* of your meals, without meat or dairy.

"Oh, fine!" we can just hear you huffing into these pages. "First you tell me to lose the white flour and rice and potatoes. Then, no sugar and no packaged foods. Now this!"

We know it sounds both shocking and nearly impossible if, like us, you've grown up eating meat, dairy and white bread at nearly every meal. That's how we learned to cook, too. But dear pals, if you want the most vibrant complexion, the most energy, the clearest eyes, the most beautiful hair, the best body, you should think seriously about changing your relationship to ground beef, pastrami and cheese.

So bear with us, please, on this quest for fabulousness, and stick one toe at a time in, if you like. But the more you know about who's staying healthy and alive longer (and looking better the whole time), the more you can no longer wave off the idea of including way, way less meat and dairy in your life.

And we haven't even mentioned all the other benefits. You spend less for groceries. Your house smells better all the time. You smell better. Your kitchen is cleaner. (No grease!) You don't have to stand at the butcher's counter for twenty minutes dithering between the tri-tip and the London broil.

Because you're not drinking that cow's milk or eating that country-fried steak, you will also be making an important contribution to a healthier planet. By slightly reducing the amount of methane gas, antibiotics and animal waste being pumped into the environment as we raise cattle for food, you've done something huge.

Is that all we have?

....

Yep, that's it. If you want billions of recipes, go online.
Go into the bookstore. Pick up any magazine, on any rack.
What we were hoping to do was share only those few that
we turn to over and over because they're easy, they're cheap,
they work, and they're as healthful as we know how to make.

Thank you for spending this time with us. We celebrate
your large and small step towards your own and your
family's health. Write to us from your kitchen table.
Send thoughts, questions, recipes, successes.

Above all, stay close.

www.deidrehall.me

Acknowledgments

First, a huge thank-you to Rainey Sealey, Jan George and Melissa Streeter for your editing help, among so many other things.

Then, a shout-out to the ever-fabulous Helen Gurley Brown, who showed us all how to change lives, hearts and minds with a well-placed *italic*.

Eternal gratitude, as always, to Rodger for all the big and little things you do that have made this possible.

And to Elise, Jane, and Dori: we love that you didn't just laugh us out the door. Thank you, girls, for being crazy with us.